Spells & Charms

Spells & Charms

52 charms and spells to help you
get the best out of life

NICOLA DE PULFORD

A GODSFIELD BOOK

First published in Great Britain in 1999
Library of Congress
Library of Congress Cataloging-in-Publication Data
Nicola de Pulford.
    Spells and charms / Nicola de Pulford.
        p.   cm.
    Includes index.

10 9 8 7 6 5 4 3 2 1

Published in 1999 by
Sterling Publishing Company, Inc.
387 Park Avenue South, New York, N.Y. 10016
© 1999 Godsfield Press
Text © 1999 Nicola de Pulford

Nicola de Pulford asserts the moral right to be identified as
the author of this work.

Distributed in Canada by Sterling Publishing
c/o Canadian Manda Group,
One Atlantic Avenue, Suite 105,
Toronto, Ontario, Canada M6K 3E7
Distributed in Australia by
Capricorn Link (Australia) Pty Ltd
P O. Box 6651, Baulkham Hills
Business Centre, NSW 2153, Australia

Printed and bound in Hong Kong

Sterling ISBN 0-8069-9915-2

Contents

Introduction

These easy-to-follow spells and charms will help you with all aspects of your life, from affairs of the heart to family matters. They will also enable you to reawaken your natural instincts and powers.

Magic has for many years been a taboo subject, supposedly practised by a handful of cranks and irrelevant to the modern world. And yet, many features of our lives, such as telephones, airplanes, and antibiotics, would once have been regarded as magical. Although science now has an explanation for many of the phenomena that once baffled us, it is

not yet able to explain all the mysteries of our world.

Most of us have little connection to nature any more but we are beginning once again to see that the spirit, body, and mind

are linked. By harnessing the life force that runs through nature and by employing the power of the mind, we can use magic to enrich our lives.

This book is inspired by the sympathetic and life-enhancing magic practised by wise women and men the world over since the earliest of times; magic should never be used to harm or to control another person.

Each spell has a list of ingredients that are readily available – the way in which you use them will imbue them with magic. Candles, oils, and certain herbs are essential to many spells so build

up a store of these. And try to work with the moon's cycle for the greatest benefit. The magic of the earth is waiting to be released and spun into spells of delight: are you ready to begin your magical journey?

In Matters of Love

Seven spells for bewitching and keeping the lover of your choice

Chapter One

Apple Pie

This delightful spell from Eastern Europe will help you attract and keep true your chosen lover. Since the earliest of times, the apple tree has been regarded as one of the most magical of trees. Its wood was used for wands to draw magic circles. Sacred to Venus, the goddess of love, the apple tree is also the Celtic Tree of Life. Perform this spell on a waxing moon and wear silk threads close to your body for forty-nine hours before you perform the spell. Threads of pink, red, and purple would be a good choice. This spell is sacred to you only, so you should work your magic in a place of peace and sanctuary.

Ingredients

A PINK CANDLE

A RED AND A GREEN APPLE

A PEN AND SLIP OF PAPER

3 BRAIDED SILK THREADS

Light the candle and, holding the apples in your outstretched hands, ask for Venus' blessing. Cut each apple in half and remove the seeds, keeping them safe for later. Write or draw on the paper the attributes of your ideal lover or the name of someone you have in mind. This should not be someone who is already in a good relationship or the spell will not work. Take one half of the green apple and one half of the red, insert the paper between them and bind together with the silk threads.

Think quietly about your wish while eating the remaining apple halves. Take the bound apple and tie it to a tree or a window casement. After twenty-one hours collect the apple and remove the threads to free the spell. Cut the apple into pieces and leave outside for the birds to eat. Keep the threads in a special place in your home. Take the paper and reserved apple seeds and plant them, remembering to give thanks to Mother Earth for her gifts. As the seeds start to grow and embark upon their journey in life, so love will come to you.

1 **On a cutting board, carefully slice both apples in half and, with the tip of your knife, take out the seeds and reserve them.**

2 **Put your message on the paper and fold it to fit neatly between the apple halves. Secure the silk threads around the apple making a web-like effect. Leave one long end free to tie the apple in your chosen place.**

3 **Affirm your intention to attract love by returning the charms to the earth. The fruits of your labor will blossom for years to come.**

Tempting Taster

Whether you have a new love or a long-term partner, this old English spell will put a zing into your relationship. A Tuesday night on the waxing moon is a good time for your ritual because Tuesday is ruled by Mars, the god of desire. Wear something red, the color of passion. This could be under-wear, or a red silk scarf or ribbon. Alcoholic drinks made from honey were common in ancient Rome and Greece and drunk in quantity at banquets. In England, mead fermented from honey and water was drunk for one lunar month following a marriage to enhance the libido.

Ingredients

A SILVER RING

2 RED CANDLES

VANILLA OIL

2 RED GLASSES

MEAD LIQUEUR

Take the silver ring in the palm of your right hand and, on a moonlit night, ask the moon to bless it. Keep it safe until you wish to perform the spell. On a Tuesday evening take a bath by candlelight, adding 3 drops of vanilla oil to the water. Massage your body with the oiled water so that you are enveloped in the wonderful aroma. Dress slowly, not forgetting a splash of red clothing. Put out the candles and transfer them to the place where you will entertain your lover. One hour before his or her arrival, take your moon-charged silver ring and run it around the rim of each glass, speaking the following words:

Let this moon-drenched ring impart
All the blessings of my heart
To the one whom I desire,
Cradled here in Mars' fire.

Do this three times and then place the ring on your finger. Fill the glasses with mead, relight the candles, and meditate on the glow of the flames as you await your partner. Do not be tempted to drink the mead on your own; it is important that you drink it with your partner for a memorable evening.

I Extend your right hand toward the moon and, with your mind, draw down her rays to give more potency to the spell.

2 Charge the glasses with your incantation. Don't drink the mead alone; it is important to partake together for a memorable evening.

Love Charm

Perform this charm at any time to beguile the partner of your dreams. A medieval magician had a good piece of advice: "If you want to be loved then you must yourself first love." Having sufficient confidence in your own powers of attraction is an important part of attracting the ideal lover. If you have doubts about yourself, this charm will help you overcome them and trust in your own abilities and attractions.

Allow yourself to open your own heart so that you are able to encompass the love of others. It is also important to decide if it is love or lust that drives your longing, and be prepared for the results!

Ingredients

A PINK CANDLE

A MIRROR

A PEN AND A PIECE OF PINK PAPER

A PHOTOGRAPH OF YOURSELF

A PINK RIBBON

*I*n a dimly lit room, light the candle so that its glow surrounds your reflection in the mirror. Concentrate your thoughts on your good qualities and your wish to start a new relationship. Breathe deeply and, as you exhale, let your fears and doubts leave your body. After a few moments, draw the image of your new love on the pink paper. Place it beside your photograph and, with the pink ribbon, lace the two together so that they both lie flat. Draw them together with the ribbon and with your mind.

Hold the joined pictures in front of the mirror so that the image is reflected back and chant:

> *My inner doubts are now set free,*
> *My heart is open come to me.*
> *Let the future joy unfold,*
> *Happiness and love untold.*

Blow out the candle and watch for any images in the mirror; you may see a different person from the one you imagine. Fold the pictures together and place them in a safe place.

I **Look deeply into your own soul, as you and your image are enveloped in a haze of candlelight, discarding all apprehension.**

2 **As you physically fuse the two pictures, draw them together with your mind and spirit.**

3 **Affirm your wish for love with the spoken words and visual revelations.**

Sky Magic

This spell can help free you from the hurt inflicted by a cruel or unfaithful partner. It combines the talismanic calligraphy of Taoist magic with Oriental sky magic, which was concerned with matters of personal joy and achieving happiness. Words written on a talisman transferred the spirit of the writer onto that talisman and enabled that person to become as one with balanced spirits. Rounded writing was used to represent the "yin" or female principle, and angular writing to represent the "yang" or male principle. Try to use the correct-shaped writing according to who inflicted the hurt upon you.

Ingredients

2 YELLOW CANDLES

ROSE OIL AND OIL BURNER

YELLOW PAPER

PEN AND RED INK

Perform this spell on a windy day under a waning moon and choose a time when you will not be disturbed. Light the candles and burn a little rose oil to create a stress-free atmosphere. Cut the yellow paper into five equal pieces, about 3 in/7.5cm by 1 in./2.5. Using red ink, write a description of the hurt inflicted upon you over four of the pieces of paper, making sure you write something on each piece. On the fifth, write your hopes for future happiness. Take your messages to a hilltop, a high-rise building, or an open beach. Feeling the power of the wind, and with your eyes closed, turn three times anticlockwise releasing each of the first four pieces of paper in turn. Hold the last between the palms of your hands and turn three times in a clockwise direction. Watch as your hopes for the future are released with the last piece of paper and become part of you.

1 **Light the oil burner and inhale the fragrance of rose oil to help your spirit return to the central path.**

2 **Write your message on the five pieces of paper. Five is the number of communication and a magical number to the Chinese.**

3 **Let the natural elements enter your spirit as the spell is liberated and the hurt you have suffered falls away from you.**

The Perfect Jewel

On a Friday, the day of Venus, and with a waxing moon, dedicate a talisman to keep love with you. A talisman is created for a specific purpose and to

attract a positive force. It is traditionally made from natural elements – crystals, stones, wood, plants, and metal – and these elements correspond to the planets, and days of the week. You might like to try making your own love jewel; many craft suppliers now provide the raw materials you will need. Alternatively, you may wish to commission a special piece from a local craftsperson.

Ingredients

GEMSTONE OR CRYSTAL
AND METAL OF YOUR CHOICE
A PETAL FROM A PINK ROSE
OR CARNATION

The following list may help with your choice of metal and stones.

DAY	PLANET	METAL	COLOR
Sunday	Sun	Gold	Orange
Monday	Moon	Silver	White
Tuesday	Mars	Iron	Red
Wednesday	Mercury	Aluminum	Yellow
Thursday	Jupiter	Tin	Purple
Friday	Venus	Copper	Blue
Saturday	Saturn	Lead	Green

Once you have chosen the appropriate components of your love jewel, wait until a Friday during a waxing moon, preferably during the month of your birth, and charge your petal with the moon's blessing. Do this by holding it in your outstretched palms and, in your mind, bringing the the moon's rays down until they engulf your hands in love. When your jewel is made, the petal should be folded in place between the stone and metal to afford extra power to the talisman. Wear the jewel at all times.

1 **Choose the most perfect flower you can find and with care remove one petal for blessing. Put the flower in a vase.**

2 **Make up the jewel or commission it. For a Friday birthday, for example, use copper, the petal, then a blue crystal or stone.**

Path of Truth

From the Native Americans, a little magic to help you find a way forward if you think your partner is cheating on you or making your life unhappy. This ritual

should be carried out on your own – peace and quiet are essential. To the Native Americans, sage was one of the gifts of the Great Spirit and it was used as a powerful purifier in many of their rituals. The Romans cleansed themselves and dressed in white before ritually harvesting sage with special silver tools. The Greeks used sage as a brain tonic. In English the word "sage" has come to mean "someone who is wise."

Ingredients

FRESH SAGE LEAVES

A POT SUITABLE FOR BURNING LEAVES IN

A FEATHER

Take a handful of sage leaves and rub them between your hands, imbuing them with your doubts and fears. Place them in the pot and take a few quiet moments to collect your thoughts. Burn the herb until it starts to smoke, taking in the pungent aroma. With your right hand, use the feather to circulate the smoke around your body. Turning clockwise, acknowledge and honor the sky and the earth spirits and the four cardinal directions – north, south, east, and west. Ask them to guide you and clear a way for you to deal with your problem. Starting at your feet, use the feather to work the smoke up your body. When you reach the top of your head, shake the feather to release any negative influences. Within a short while you will think of three questions to ask your partner, and the truth will become apparent.

1 Bruise the fresh sage leaves in the palms of your hands to release the cleansing fragrance of this potent herb.

2 With a feather of your choice, encourage the smoke from the burner to cleanse your fears.
3 Concentrate and feel the clarity coming to your brain as the feather disperses any blocking energies.

The Flower of Venus

This Romany spell will help you to charm the partner of your dreams. The Gypsies are a people without nationality or written history. Forced to leave India in the first millennium A.D., they migrated to Persia. According to tradition, the first rose,

the flower of Venus, was brought to life in the Garden of Persia by the rays of the rising sun. Like the Gypsies, its seeds have spread throughout the world. For this spell, the thorns should be plucked from the rose stem because they are identified with the phallus. This, however, is a spell for love, not carnal desire.

Ingredients

2 PINK CANDLES

A LONG-STEMMED, DEEP-PINK, SCENTED ROSE

A PEN AND SCROLL OF PAPER

GREEN RIBBON

Perform this spell on a Friday night during the new moon's cycle, picking a time when you won't be disturbed. In a dimly lit room, light the candles and inhale the rose's scent as you watch the candle flames turn to a gentle pink. When you are relaxed, write about or sketch your ideal partner on the paper. Wrap the scroll tightly around the top of the rose stem and cut off the bottom of the stem that sticks out of the scroll. Place the cut stem at right angles to the scroll and bind it in place with green ribbon, thinking loving thoughts as you do so. Place in your freezer or refrigerator. Look again into the candle flames, seeing yourself and your love in contentment. After twenty-four hours, retrieve the rose figure and unbind the green ribbon to release the spell. Bury the rose and the scroll, asking for the blessing of Venus.

1 Take the perfumed long-stemmed rose and remove any thorns. Write all the qualities you wish to attract in a partner on the paper.
2 Scroll the paper around the rose and remove the protruding stem. Attach it at right angles to the scroll with the ribbon.

3 Keep a picture of your love in your mind as you make your entreaty to the goddess Venus and return the gifts to the earth.

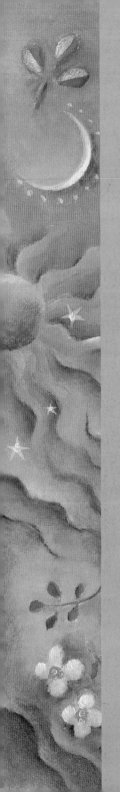

Peaches and Cream

A selection of spells to add
a little magic to your
beauty routine and to improve
your spiritual and physical energy

Chapter Two

Enlightenment From the

Native Americans, this spiritual journey will help to put your mind and

body back into balance. The everyday worries of life often take a toll on

our immune system, and this in turn can manifest itself as a physical

illness. Central to Native American

belief was the idea that all life is part of

a sacred hoop or circle, uniting both

the natural and the spirit world.

Modern society and city life have divorced the spirit world from the

natural world and separated us from our roots in Mother Earth. By

strengthening the spirit, both body and mind will become more balanced.

Ingredients

THE FOUR ELEMENTS OR SYMBOLS FOR THEM

3 SAGE LEAVES

*I*deally this ritual should be performed in the open air at noon, with the four elements – earth, air, fire, and water – naturally present. If this is not possible, use substitute flowers or symbols; or a little soil for the earth; an incense stick for air; a yellow candle for fire; some spring water. Place these in a circle and sit in the middle. Purify your face and hands by wiping them with the sage, then clasp your hands, close your eyes, and let your thoughts drift away. Open your ears and listen to the elements and nature around you. With your mind's eye, become part of the water, and feel the warm earth in your hand and the soft caress of the wind on your face. Feel the harmony and enjoy being at one with the natural world around you. Use this ritual at any time to restore balance and harmony to your life.

1 **Find a secluded spot outdoors and indulge yourself in the elements. Alternatively at home, sit with symbols of the elements around you.**

2 **As you cleanse your face and hands with the sage, imagine a waterfall as it cascades to the earth, glinting with dazzling sunlight.**

3 **While you relax and meditate, feel the breath of air touching your face, linking you to all other living beings, and let peace enter your spirit.**

Comfrey and Care

Ease aches and pains and restore the spirit with this spell based on old

English traditions. Common comfrey was

known to medieval herbalists as "knitbone"

or "boneset" – the powdered root was

made into a paste with water and used in

the same way as plaster of Paris. The

common name comes from the Latin *conferre* meaning, "to bring

together." Comfrey baths for women were also popular before

marriage to "restore virginity." The following routine can be repeated

every few days for effective relief.

Ingredients

COMFREY OIL

COMFREY CREAM

2 PIECES OF WILLOW, ABOUT 4FT. 6IN./1.35M. LONG

WHITE RIBBON

Choose a quiet time during the waning moon and run a bath to which you have added a few drops of comfrey oil. If you have a specific area of pain, rub a little comfrey cream into it with clockwise circular motions, concentrating on bringing out the pain and then shaking it away from you. Put the pieces of willow lengthwise in the bath and place yourself between them, holding one in each hand; relax. Close your eyes and feel the warmth envelop your whole body. Imagine the aches and pains traveling along threads in your inner self and out through your fingertips into the willow. Dry yourself and remove the willow from the water. Form the willow into two circles by bending it around and binding the ends together with the white ribbon. Step into the willow circles one at a time and pass them all the way up the length of your body and back down to the ground. Put the willow circles outside your home for twenty-four hours, then release the ribbons to free the spell.

1 **Collect the ingredients and make sure the bathroom is warm and comfortable before running the water. Apply the comfrey cream and add a few drops of the oil.**

2 **As you enter the bath, hold the willow in a relaxed floating manner, and let your mind do the traveling.**
3 **Tie the willow in two circles and close your eyes as you move them up and down your body. Untie the ribbons outside.**

29

Lavender and Love

For a special occasion, follow the Romans' example and use this hair tonic to lift your spirits and attract attention. The species of lavender most widely used in past times was French lavender, *Lavandula stoechas*. English lavender, *L. angustifolia*, the hardier species, has been used as a cosmetic and strewing herb since the twelfth century. The oil, derived from the floral part of the plant, is extremely versatile. It can both soothe and revive, and so will respond to the body's needs. In this charm, any fragrant lavender flowers, fresh or dried, may be used.

Chapter Two Peaches and Cream

Ingredients

A SMALL ORANGE VELVET SACHET
OR SQUARE OF ORANGE VELVET
FRESH OR DRIED LAVENDER FLOWERS
A LOCK OF YOUR HAIR
LAVENDER OIL
A LENGTH OF BLUE CORD

Before you leave home for a special occasion, allow enough time to perform this spell. Take the orange sachet or square of orange velvet and place five fresh lavender flowers or five pinches of dried lavender in it. Orange is the color of joy and optimism. Place the lock of hair in the sachet and as you do so chant:

Spirit of my soul unite
With this herb of sweet delight.
Carry us throughout the day,
Ease the path along the way.

Wash your hair. Then dilute 5–10 drops of lavender oil in a glass of water and use this as the final rinse. Sprinkle a few drops of the oil mixture onto the sachet, to strengthen your charm, and knot the parcel five times with blue cord. Blue is the color of the spirit and represents protection. Carry the charm close to you all day. Your intoxicating fragrance and charm will heighten as the day progresses.

1 Put the lock of hair in the sachet with the lavender and give it a shake to mix the ingredients.

2 Think of the words you have just spoken as you wash your hair and dress it with lavender oil.

3 Five is the number of sex, so your finished charm – with its five knots – may attract a host of surprises.

31

Aromatic Study

Follow this Eastern ritual of magic and massage for a sensuous and uplifting experience. It will heighten your own and your partner's physical and spiritual well-being and could lead to an exciting evening when anything might happen! In the East, some belief systems, such as the Tantra, consider making love to be a sacred experience. The physical act was considered as a sign of spiritual union, allied with the principle of creation. The hours between 7 p.m. and midnight are an ideal time to practice this ritual.

Ingredients

4 RED CANDLES

A SILVER DISH CONTAINING SPICED FINGER FOOD

VERMOUTH

3 DROPS EACH OF ROSE OTTO AND
SANDALWOOD OIL, DILUTED IN 4 TSP. OF BASE OIL

In a dimly lit room, light the candles with your partner and place one in each corner. Place the food and vermouth in the center of the room and spread cushions all around it. Sitting cross-legged, close your eyes and, for at least ten minutes, free your mind of all thoughts. Partake together of a little vermouth and food, leaving some for later. Put some oil on the palms of your hands and begin to caress each other's feet and hands. Then massage each other in turn, using slow-flowing movements, paying particular attention to the back of the knees and neck, the insides of the thighs and arms, and the ears. Endeavor to give each other at least ten full minutes of bliss before moving on to other things! Finally, consume the remaining food and a toast of vermouth and give thanks for the joy you have given each other.

1 **Prepare the room in silence, giving yourselves time to reflect until your minds are free.**
2 **Feed each other the food and drink. This will heighten your awareness and desire to share in the pleasures of life.**

3 **Begin the massage with the left foot, stroking firmly with both hands from the toes toward the ankle, and then returning with a light stroke.**

Easing the Load

A spell to help your weight-loss program and to improve your inner health. The spiritual state of a person is as important as the physical when embarking on a diet. It is vital to believe in yourself, so when beginning your diet, take ten minutes every day when you are completely alone, preferably outdoors, and spend it indulging in your own

thoughts. You will find it easier to stick to a sensible eating routine or slimming diet if you work this spell at the same time. Start it on a Sunday morning, since this is the day for good fortune and hope.

Ingredients

12 DIFFERENT–COLORED SILK SCARFS,
   ONE OF WHICH SHOULD BE YELLOW OR GOLDEN

A ROLLING PIN

1OZ./25G FRESH OR DRIED DILL

1PT/500ML BOILING WATER

A SECRET DIARY

Wrap the silk scarfs, one at a time, around the rolling pin, finishing with the golden or yellow one. Place the rolling pin in a dark place; this is a symbolic representation of you. Steep the dill in the boiling water and drink half a cup before each meal. Once a day take a long walk and as you go try to see things around you that you would not normally notice. When you get home, write down in the diary your observations and how you feel. After one week, take the top scarf from the rolling pin and wear it close to your skin for the day. In the evening, tie it in a bow in a prominent place in your home. Each week remove one scarf until you achieve your desired weight. Keep the diary going for as long as possible.

1 **Work on a waning moon, and as you wrap the last golden scarf around the rolling pin, remind yourself that yellow represents achievement.**

2 **Make a ritual of infusing the dill and try not to miss it out before a meal, even if you are pressed for time.**

3 **When writing in the diary, be honest and let all your feelings flow onto the paper. This will help you achieve your goal.**

Frankincense and Thyme

As we get older many of us try to combat the ravages of time with expensive creams and lotions; we waste time worrying about aging instead of enjoying life. This spell

may help you to keep your skin looking as young as possible and encourage you to grow older gracefully. Frankincense is a wonderfully fragrant and spiritual oil ideal for use in meditation, and thyme makes for an excellent tonic. A full appreciation of life itself is a wonderful healer, so make use of your time and enjoy yourself with this magical reminder of Mother Nature's great gifts.

Ingredients

THYME OIL AND OIL BURNER

A THYME PLANT OR PLANTS

FRANKINCENSE OIL

UNPERFUMED BASE CREAM

Start your regime by burning a little thyme oil at the beginning of the day. Let its essence fill the house and make yourself comfortable. Imagine you are walking on a creeping carpet of wild thyme. As its sweet perfume reaches your senses, you hear the faint sound of bees collecting this wonderful flavor to turn into honey. Examine the good and bad things about your life, and make a pledge to go forward and achieve some of the little things you always promised yourself you would do. Put your thyme plant in a prominent position, or plant a variety of thyme, if you have a garden. Each day, spend a few moments with the plant to reflect on your pledge and the goals you have set yourself. Mix a few drops of frankincense oil with the base cream and apply lovingly to your face each night before bed.

1 Sit in a chair or lie on the floor and let the essence of thyme stimulate your brain as you appreciate all the good things in your life.

2 If it helps, make a list of all those things you wish to change, and those you want to attract.

3 To appreciate fully the aroma of your thyme plant, gently bruise a leaf with your fingers, as you reflect on your new path.

Healing Meditation

An aromatic meditation to restore your balance with the natural world. Vetiver oil is extracted from the fragrant root of this tall, grasslike plant and has a rich and deeply earthy aroma. Known as the oil of tranquillity it is renowned for its ability to bring people back down to earth and for helping people to get their lives back on an even keel after a bad experience or shock. The dandelion is the flower of survival and is present in folk and magical tradition all over the world; always springing up in unexpected places, its power to foil the avid gardener is legendary.

Ingredients

A BOWL OF SAND

A BUNCH OF DANDELIONS

VETIVER OIL

A COTTON PAD

A good comfortable chair in which your feet can touch the ground is ideal for this meditation. Position the chair so that it is facing south and place the bowl of sand so that your bare feet can rest in it. Put the dandelions in a glass vase in front of the chair where you can comfortably see them. Put 2 drops of vetiver oil on the cotton pad and sit in the chair with your feet resting on the sand. Wave the pad just in front of you and inhale the aroma with long, deep breaths and think of Mother Earth. Let your toes squeeze slowly into the sand and visualize your inner self enveloped in a warm brown robe that enriches your life with fertility. As you do this, remember that you are part of the inexorable circle of life and that the sacred earth needs your care and attention as much as you need hers.

1 Collect the dandelions, and fill a large bowl with sand. A plastic dish–washing bowl is a good choice.

2 Focus your gaze on the flowers as you let your mind drift with the wonderful scent.

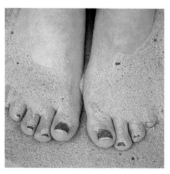

3 As you feel the heaviness of the sand around your feet, close your eyes and let your whole body become as one with it.

Time and Travel

A selection of charms and spells
to help ease your path through
the physical and spiritual world

Chapter Three

River Spell

A charm from Finland to attract good fortune and luck on vacation, whether at home or abroad. Magic and shamanism played a huge part in the lives of Finnish people, both in material and intellectual aspects, right up to the twentieth century. The power of the Finnish magicians was renowned and often feared by those in authority. Most everyday tasks were accompanied by chants

and incantations that were meant to protect and enhance life. This charm can be performed close to any fresh water, such as a river, spring, or lake – the water will help the magic to flow.

Ingredients

A FEW HANDFULS OF GRASS

2 STICKS ABOUT 1FT./30CM LONG

A CRYSTAL OF YOUR CHOICE

NATURAL WOOL

Find a natural water source, such as a river, spring, or lake, and collect a few handfuls of grass and two stoutish sticks. Sit down and place your chosen crystal in front of you. Fashion a little doll from the grasses, using the wool to hold the figure together. Be as artistic and creative as you can, and put all your feelings into the work, so that the finished article gives you joy and satisfaction. Place the doll next to the crystal and take the two sticks into your hands. Tap them together to produce a rhythmic beat and chant the following:

> *Water sprites receive my gift*
> *And grant good chance with every wish.*
> *Let my life flow strong and pure,*
> *A bubbling spring of joy and strength.*

Hold the crystal in your left hand and float the figure away on the water. Close your eyes and meditate for a few moments before departing.

1 **Divide your bundle of grass, into two bunches. Bend the first bunch in half to form the head, body, and legs of the doll. Place the rest at right angles and secure with a piece of grass or string.**

2 **Try to make the beat of your sticks fit to the rhythm of the water source.**
3 **When you chant, focus your gaze on the crystal and repeat the words of the spell several times. Pick up the crystal, and gently place the figure in the water.**

Angelic Aid

A practical remedy to help alleviate travel sickness and to invoke the help of the gods for a pleasant journey. Travel sickness combined with nervousness about

making a particular trip can be debilitating and spoil what might be the vacation of a lifetime. Having a peaceful mind and feeling relaxed about the trip will be the first step towards solving the problem, and a magical ritual may focus your mind and ease the way. If you are traveling with others, it could be helpful to get them involved – a fear shared is a fear halved. Start a few days before your departure.

Ingredients

A KEY

A SYMBOL OF YOUR DESTINATION

ANGELICA SEEDS

4 DROPS EACH OF ANGELICA, MELISSA,

   PEPPERMINT, AND GINGER OIL,

DILUTED IN 5 TSP. OF SWEET ALMOND OIL

A few days before you begin your journey, point the key in the direction that you intend to travel, next to the symbol of your destination. The key represents your mode of transportation – you could also add an appropriate model to the arrangement, such as a model car or airplane. Form a circle of angelica seeds around the objects making sure the circle is complete – this will keep the contents safe.

Each day before you depart spend ten minutes near your symbols, asking for the gods' blessing and visualizing yourself traveling in the bubble of a protective white light. Try to see yourself as part of the new landscape. If you are performing this spell as part of a group, form a circle and join hands. Use the oils as a tonic against sickness on your journey; just inhale the aroma and dab a little behind the ears to ward off nausea.

**1 Ensure you have the ingredients for this spell in good time. Rushing around to find them at the last minute will add to your nervousness.
2 In a safe place make a circle of angelica seeds in close single file around your symbols.**

3 Mix the oils before you depart. Put them in a plastic bottle for traveling and use them as often as necessary.

Time Tricks

Some ancient Greek number magic to help you find the right day and time to work your spells. Choosing the right time to perform magic has always been an

important part of the craft. You can also use this magic to find out your personal number and the attributes and qualities it reveals. Pythagoras, the great Greek mathematician, was also a psychic and magician who believed that "all things are numbers." He was assassinated by the authorities because of his great powers, but his powerful secrets were passed down by word of mouth or in coded scripts.

Ingredients

PEN AND PAPER

NUMERIC VALUE OF LETTER

1	2	3	4	5	6	7	8	9
A	B	C	D	E	F	G	H	I
J	K	L	M	N	O	P	Q	R
S	T	U	V	W	X	Y	Z	

Mon	Tues	Wed	Thurs	Fri	Sat	Sun
1	2	3	4	5	6	7

ATTRIBUTES OF PERSONAL NUMBERS

1 Pioneer – courageous but also lonely

2 Harmony – passive people linked to psychic powers

3 Joy – lucky and possibly extravagant people

4 Loyal – hardworking people who pay a high price for success

5 Freedom – radical people who sometimes find relationships hard

6 Sincerity – people who are loved but sometimes conceited

7 Spirituality – educated people who are sometimes aloof

8 Organization – prosperous but sometimes pessimistic people

9 Intellectuals – idealists who can be jealous

Following the chart opposite and using the full name by which you are most commonly called, add up the numbers that correspond to the letters of your name. If the total adds up to more than one digit, keep adding them together until you are left with one digit. For example, "Nicola" is 5 + 9 + 3 + 6 + 3 + 1 = 27, 2 + 7 = 9, so 9 is the personal number for Nicola. To choose a day to work magic, divide the total of your added numbers by 7. In the example above you would divide 27 by 7, which is 3 with 6 left over. Apply the leftover number to the days of the week opposite – in this case 6 becomes Saturday. If the number divides exactly by 7, 7 is the number you should use. If you know the time of your birth, then try doing your spells at this time on your lucky day.

Elizabeth

5 + 12 + 9 + 26 + 1 + 2 + 5 + 20 + 8

= 88

8 + 8 = 16

1 + 6 = 7

Personal number = 7

Lucky spell day 7 = Sunday

47

Astral Travel

A gentle spell to open your mind, body, and spirit to the possibilities of life outside our normal conscious state. The existence of different energies and forces has been debated for decades. Even science has investigated some of these possibilities; using special techniques, Semyon Kirlian was able to photograph the auras that surround people and plants. His experiments also found that the aura of a healthy livng plant was bigger and brighter than that of a cut plant. Patience is required to open up the mind to higher states of consciousness and clairvoyancy, so if you do not succeed the first time keep trying.

Ingredients

3 CANDLES ANOINTED WITH
A COMBINATION OF 3, 5, OR
7 ESSENTIAL OILS OF YOUR CHOICE

*I*t may be helpful to do this exercise with a friend or partner. Light the oiled candles and turn out all other lights. Place them so that you can lie in the center of them. Close your eyes and gently relax, releasing your brain from everyday trivia. Project your imagination onto the ocean's horizon; let the misty blue hues engulf you and lead you on to a path of air. Travel on slowly and note all that you see. Accept all that you are offered but do not try to communicate. As you go along, you may hear conversation, your senses may be aroused, and fragrances may draw you forward. Go with them, glancing up and down so as to miss nothing. As the blue fades away, slowly begin your return to earth and, as you finally reach this world, open your eyes and stretch. Then join hands with your companion and give thanks.

1 **When you have chosen your combination of essential oils, mix a few drops of each in a little bowl.**

2 **To anoint the candles, dip the wick into the oil mixture, then dab oil along the length, rubbing it gently into the candle.**

3 **Having lit the candles, concentrate on their glow and set them in place. Then return to meditate in the center of the ring of candles.**

First Voyage

If you are cautious about making a first voyage, create a special talisman in the African tradition to attract benevolent influences and bring you good speed. In times of danger or worry, we often carry or wear some lucky object, or

we might find or buy something that becomes lucky for us later on. Losing a treasured charm can cause seemingly irrational fears, and at the back of your mind there is the subconscious belief that part of you has been somehow lost. Confirm your belief and set your mind at rest by dedicating this special talisman to keep the gods on your side.

Ingredients

A LONG, THIN PIECE OF BROWN SILK

FRESH OR DRIED VERVAIN

A NEEDLE

SOME THREAD

3 SMALL SHELLS

*I*t is important that the making of this talisman is treated as a focussed meditation, so choose a quiet time and place in which to work. See it as a task into which you can manifest the protection you wish to receive and give it your undivided concentration. As you work, feel the spirit of the ingredients and harness their energy. The color brown represents a protective shield, the shells are a symbol of the traveler; and vervain is the most sacred of herbs for protection. Lay the silk flat and sprinkle it with vervain leaves. Roll in the edges so that you have a long tube, and then sew or bind its length. Attach a shell at each end and one in the middle and wear the silk around your waist for twenty-four hours before the journey and during it.

1 Lay the silk flat and sprinkle the length with vervain leaves, keeping them in the central portion of the cloth.

2 Roll the edges in so you have a long tube shape. Sew or bind its length and attach a shell at each end and one in the middle.

3 Wear the silk around your waist for twenty four hours before the journey and during it.

Future Thoughts

Encourage your powers of clairvoyance and perception with this simple

meditation. Foretelling the future is a natural human concern, and

divination in all its forms has been with us

throughout history, continued by the few

who have the gift of "the sight." Although,

on the whole, clairvoyants are born with

their gift, there are numerous examples of

ordinary people suddenly becoming aware

of the future, sometimes after a traumatic experience or illness. It may

be that most of us have never tried to develop this gift even though the

facility is there, waiting to emerge.

Ingredients

A BOWL OF SPRING WATER

A WHITE CANDLE

Do not be in a hurry to try out your own powers of clairvoyance. Think about what you are going to do for a while and start by teaching your mind to concentrate on an object for short periods of time. Wait until there is a full moon to give as much power as possible to your endeavor. Place the bowl of water where the moonlight illuminates it; this could be inside on a moonlit windowsill, or in the open, if you prefer. Light the candle and position it so that its flame flickers on the surface of the water. Concentrate on the pool of water, emptying your mind of all conscious thoughts. Allow your inner mind to do the seeing; you may find this takes you in new directions and gives you an altogether different perspective on life.

1 **The magnificent full moon is the most potent to work by; she is the queen of the night and represents the inner soul of humankind.**

2 **Ensure that you are warm and comfortable and will not be distracted by outside influences when you choose a place for your meditation.**

Happy Journey

A ritual to perform before you depart on any journey to ensure its

success and your peace of mind. Because of the beliefs that crystal con-

nects heaven and earth and that a circle

embodies completeness, crystal spheres have

come to be the most magical of divinatory

objects. Crystal quartz is found in many parts

of the world and is used in rituals in many

different cultures. You do not need to spend a fortune on a state-of-the-

art crystal ball: a small glass or beryl sphere, or even a paperweight, is

ideal for this spell and will work just as well if your own input is sincere.

Ingredients

A SMALL CRYSTAL SPHERE

A BOWL OF SPRING WATER

SALT

A YELLOW CANDLE

When ready to undertake your trip, go to a quiet place and put the crystal sphere in the bowl of spring water. Watch the ripples as they spread, and then become calm, symbolizing a speedy and comfortable voyage. Sprinkle some salt over the crystal to represent the stability of the earth. Light the candle and drip some hot wax onto the water; as it sets, it symbolizes land and indicates your safe arrival.

The shape formed by the wax on the water may be representative of some feature of your journey. Extinguish the candle and repeat the words:

So as you rise above the earth,
lift me from adversity.

Lift the crystal from the water and dry it gently. Wrap it carefully and take it with you.

1 Choose a glass or silver-colored bowl in which to place the crystal, and, before you begin your work, polish the bowl until it sparkles.

2 As you sprinkle the salt over the crystal, close your eyes and relax, meditating for a few moments until you are calm. Then light the candle.

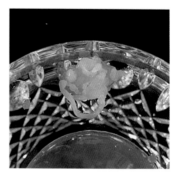

3 When the candle has burned down for a few moments, allow the wax to drop onto the surface of the water.

Hearth and Home

A little gentle magic to smooth
even the most difficult situations
and to keep your family and home
in harmony

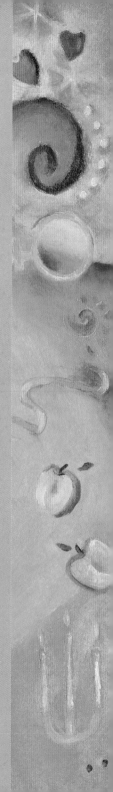

Chapter Four

Home Wisdom

A little Celtic wisdom to keep your home in balance at all times. In the past, protecting the home was of paramount importance; it was the place where people were most at ease and, consequently, at their most vulnerable. In many parts of the world even building materials are chosen with great care for their magical properties. For example, in the old days, trees bearing thorns were not used to build a house because it would

bode ill for the inhabitants. It was also important to bring the protection of Mother Nature into the home and to reestablish the connection with her while in an artificial environment.

Ingredients

7 ACORNS

A NEEDLE

RED THREAD

A LONG TWIG OF WILLOW

2 TWIGS OF ROWAN

IVY

RED RIBBONS

Make a special trip to the country with the whole family to collect the natural ingredients (listed above) needed for this spell. During this adventure, be at one with Mother Nature and treat her with the respect that she deserves by giving thanks for her gifts. At home, thread the acorns onto a length of red thread. These perfect fruits, with their beautifully designed carrying cups, remind us that even the smallest of things can blossom into great miracles. Bind the willow into a circle to represent the circle of life. Bind the rowan into a cross for the crossroads of life. Tie the ivy in a garland to represent the full joy of life and decorate it with red ribbons. When your work is done, spend a quiet moment in meditation and then tie your treasures in the furthest corners of your home.

1 Use a needle to thread the acorns onto the red thread, knotting the first one in place. The needle will pass easily through the nut part of the acorn, leaving the carrying cups in place.

2 A thin sappy endpiece of willow will bend easily into a circle. As you bind the wood, feel its texture and form.

3 Long or short pieces of ivy can be used. They will naturally intertwine to make a garland when put in position, and can be secured in place with a little thread.

Crystal and Candle

For those who feel nervous when they are at home alone, this ritual will disperse your foreboding. If outside influences stay with you indoors, or you are a nervous person,

this spell may also be useful in pinpointing the reason for your anxiety. If there is an object in the home that upsets you, you can remove it. Sometimes there is no obvious reason for hidden fears, they are just a reaction to the unknown. If the chosen oils do not appeal to you, try one or a blend of the following: bergamot, clary sage, frankincense, juniper berry, melissa, neroli, rose otto, or ylang ylang.

Ingredients

A WHITE CANDLE

LAVENDER AND CAMOMILE OIL

AGATE CRYSTAL

Perform this ritual with a waning moon at the time of day when you feel most uneasy. Turn on all the lights in the house even if it is daylight. Anoint the candle with the oils and light it. Place the candle as near as you can to the center of your home. Sit beside it, holding the crystal in your hands. Feel the light and aroma from the candle passing into your body and filling it. Open all the doors and windows. Working clockwise around your home, go to each room and, with the crystal in your outstretched hand, draw out all the negative energy. Shake it out of the window in each room and release the negative spirits. Finish your ritual at the main entrance of the house, walking out backward and turning three times before shaking the crystal in the air to complete the ritual. Wash the crystal and keep it safe.

I **Make sure the crystal is clean and bright before you start this spell. Place the crystal in the palm of your hand and cup the other hand over it.**

2 **Concentrate hard as you work your way around the house. At the end, hold the crystal under running water for about half a minute before you dry it and store away safely.**

Kitchen Lore

Follow this ritual and make your kitchen a place of joy and harmony. The kitchen has always been a traditional source of magic in many countries, and a

remains a focal room in many homes. Creating a balanced atmosphere in your kitchen will not only provide a welcoming and relaxing space, it will also make it an ideal location for the preparation of magic. Qi (pronounced "chee") is a positive energy force that sustains all living things; it sometimes becomes blocked and creates the wrong atmosphere. This ritual will help restore the positive flow of Qi in your kitchen.

Ingredients

PENDULUM OR KEY

LENGTH OF CORD

SELECTION OF CHINESE SPICES

SHINY METAL BOWL

BOILING WATER

To check if your kitchen has a negative flow of Qi, work in daylight and in peace. Thread the pendulum or key onto your cord and hold it in front of you; it will swing regularly as you walk. Starting from the center of the room, walk outward in a clockwise direction, covering the whole area. If the pendulum stops, swings, or pulls in an erratic manner, there is an energy blockage. Note where this happens. To restore harmony, start by placing spices in the metal bowl in the center of the space. Then pour boiling water over them so that aromatic steam rises up out of the bowl. Place a mirror on the wall that is opposite the problem area to reverse the flow of negative energy. Arrange as many plants as you can in the space. You will immediately notice the difference as negative energy is transformed to positive, and blocked energy is released.

I **Make sure that the key hangs vertically on the cord, with about a 40cm drop beneath it.**

2 **At first the aroma will be quite pungent as you pour boiling water over the spices, but the odor will soon fade to a pleasing scent.**

Sweet Dreams

Follow the wisdom of traditional folklore to avoid restless nights and implement good sleeping patterns. Insomnia is an all too frequent problem for many people. It can be caused by anxiety or excitement, emotional stress, an over-active mind, exhaustion, or sleeping in a stuffy environment. Being tired is not  always related to the amount of sleep you get; it can also be related to the quality of your sleep and nutritional imbalance. Developing a routine, along with a harmonious environment, sensible diet, and a little magic thrown in, can greatly improve the situation.

Ingredients

1OZ/25G DRIED VERVAIN

1PT/500ML BOILING WATER

7 FEATHERS, AT LEAST 6IN./15.5CM IN LENGTH

A NEEDLE

SOME THREAD

LAVENDER OIL

about half an hour before you plan to retire, make an infusion by adding boiling water to vervain and let it steep for about ten minutes. While you are waiting, lay the feathers horizontally on a flat surface, one above the other. Bind them together at each end, leaving a space between each one so that they make a ladder effect. As you work, chant quietly:

Lift my mind above the day,
dispel my thoughts and lead the way,
Charm my body into sleep,
spell my soul the peace to keep.

Drink a cup of vervain tea and hang the charm above your bed. Make sure the room is well aired and put a dab of lavender oil on the light bulb while you prepare for bed. Lie in bed and let the aroma of lavender pervade your senses. Focus your mind on the feathers and on the birds they came from. Walk your mind up the charm-ladder to soar to the heavens with the birds. Sweet dreams.

1 Lay the feathers so that the quill ends alternate, down the row, then secure first one end then the other to the thread.

2 As you drink the vervain tea close your eyes and let the words of the chant drift through your mind.

Fertility Rite

A sympathetic and safe spell that gives nature a chance to work her own magic. Since the beginning of time, men and women have practiced fertility magic.

Today, we no longer have much contact with the natural cycle of the seasons and the abundant fertility of the earth. The month of February during a new moon is the time to start this ritual; this is when the natural world starts to restore herself. To aid nature in this rite, avoid too much alcohol and high-acid foods and fruits. Green is the color of fertility, while white is for beginning a new phase.

Ingredients

A HOLLOW EGG, SUCH AS
  A CARDBOARD EASTER EGG
A WHITE CANDLE
A POMEGRANATE
A GREEN POUCH

In the evening, open the hollow egg and place it on a windowsill where it can receive the moonlight. Make yourself comfortable and light the white candle. Concentrate on the candle's glow and try to atune yourself to your natural senses. Peel the pomegranate and eat the juicy pulp around each seed – extracting them one by one. Reserve one pomegranate seed and let it dry overnight. The next morning, place the seed in the egg and close it. Each day, until the full moon, take a walk and collect two small natural items, such as a stone, leaf, or seed. Place these items in a green pouch and sleep with the parcel under your pillow. During your walks, take note of the living creatures all around you and wish yourself to be included in this miracle of nature. When the moon is at its fullest, leave the egg open over-night. The next day, close the egg and place it in a dark drawer; if you need to, do the same thing on the next full moon.

1 **Do not hurry when you eat the pomegranate. Savor the texture, the color, and the taste of its seeds, as well as the fruit's magical form.**

2 **You may like to choose a special color for the egg shape. An easy way to do this is to cover it with silver or colored foil.**

3 **Take care and pride in choosing the natural items to fit into your green pouch – look for special colors and unusual shapes.**

Guardian Spell

A spell to give strength and protection to your home and family, and to help connect you with the natural world. This spell should be repeated quarterly on Samhaine (October 31st), Imbolc (February 2nd), Beltaine (April 30th), and Lagnasad (August 1st). These are the traditional main "sabbats" or meetings of witches and are the ideal times for casting off the old and welcoming in the new, as well as for celebrating the cycle of the seasons. Cast your spell at these important crossroads in the year to uplift your spirits and encourage a sense of unity in your home.

Ingredients

FIRE OR 5 RED CANDLES TO REPRESENT FIRE

GREENERY AND FLOWERS APPROPRIATE
  TO THE TIME OF YEAR

SYMBOLS OF YOU OR YOUR FAMILY

A CUP OF SPRING WATER

I f you have a hearth use it as your center, otherwise use the lighted candles or a make a small fire in the yard. Go out as a family to gather the greenery and, as you do so, swap stories of any associations that are connected with your choices and give thanks for the earth's gifts. Each of the sabbats has its own "sigil" (symbol) and you should fashion your greenery into a garland of the appropriate shape. Decorate it with symbols of you and/or your family, and then stand around it joining hands for a moment's silence. Pass the water clockwise to each person in the circle, taking a sip and asking for a blessing in the coming quarter-year. Leave the sigil in your home for twenty-four hours and then hang it on the door of the main entrance to the house.

WITCHES' SABBATS

Imbolc

Beltaine

Lagnasad

Samhaine

1 This sigil for Beltaine was made by tying together two twigs of the correct shape. Then ivy and honeysuckle were twined around the twigs and flowers laced on top.

2 Make your journey to collect the ingredients a happy one involving all members of the family.

Child Support

This spell will help you deal with your feelings when your children leave home. Suddenly finding yourself in an empty house after years spent dedicated to

the needs of others is bound to leave a void in your life. The strong emotions this can stir often make you seem overprotective and meddling, rather than caring and loving. The last thing you want to do is destroy the love that has been nurtured over the years. Sending your love with them, while at the same time forging a path for them to follow with ease. This can only strengthen the bonds that join you and your children.

Ingredients

SILVER CANDLE

EVENING PRIMROSE OIL

A LOCK OF YOUR HAIR

A LOCK OF YOUR CHILD'S HAIR

SOME SILVER RIBBON

The evening primrose is the flower of silent love. Burn the oil in the house as often as possible to help ease your fears. Since you wish to let go of some of your feelings, work with the waning moon. In a quiet place, anoint the silver candle with some evening primrose oil and light it. Silver is the color of intuition and latent potential. Think lovingly of your child as you entwine the two locks of hair together. Then bind them all the way down with the silver ribbon. As you do so, wish your child good luck on whichever path he or she chooses to follow and make a promise that you will always be there if needed. Kiss your silver parcel and then cut it in half. Kiss both halves, then keep them safely together in a special place.

1 Lace the locks of hair around each other and hold them in your thumb and forefinger. Wrap the ribbon lengthwise around the hair and secure with a little sticking tape.

2 Feel your love and support reaching out to your children as their essence is in your hands and you place the parcel to your lips.

Golden Opportunities

Whether you need inspiration in your current work, a new job, or some extra money and luck, these spells will help you climb the ladder to success

Chapter Five

Apple and Cider

From old England, a charm to get your business or job off to a good start. The apple tree was known to the Celts as the "Tree of Life," and was also sacred to the Greeks and Romans. In Norse legend, golden apples kept

the gods eternally youthful, while for Native Americans, it represented the "Tree of Heaven." Apple trees were planted to ward off evil spirits and, when the fruit was harvested, a few were always left to appease good spirits. Both the fruit and wood of the tree have been used in spells. Start this charm when you get a new job or wish a business to be successful.

Ingredients

5 ORANGE CANDLES

AN APPLE TWIG

A SMALL KNIFE

AN APPLE

A BOWL

A SYMBOL OF YOUR WORK

CIDER

On a Friday night, place the lit candles in a large circle. Use orange candles as orange is the color of optimism and determination. Put all the other ingredients in the center of the circle. Take the apple twig and draw an inner circle on the floor, working in a clockwise direction. You must remain within this magic circle to perform your spell. With the knife, cut the apple into 22 pieces; the number 22 incorporates all the magic of other numbers.

Drop each piece of apple into a bowl, wishing for luck in your venture as you do so. Place the symbol you have chosen to represent your work on top and sprinkle with a little cider. Stir the pot in a clockwise direction. As you put in effort, so your life will bear fruit. Close your eyes and wish for success before drinking a toast of cider.

1 Make sure that your circle is big enough to work in, taking care that the candles are safely placed.

2 Remaining within the ring of candles, chop the apple into 22 pieces, more or less equally sized.

3 Pour yourself a glass of cider, close your eyes and make your wish before finishing all the cider in the glass.

75

Sun - blessed

This is a spell for inspiration when new ideas seem hard to come by and you seem to have a mental block. St. John's Wort *(Hypericum perforatum)* has small

sunlike flowers and grows in the wild across Europe. Traditionally gathered at midsummer, this flower had magic that was said to last a long time, acting as a tonic, and protecting against bad omens. The Greeks believed that the odor produced by glands in its leaves is strong enough to drive away evil spirits. *H. perforatum* is easy to grow and offers magical delight in any garden or window box.

Ingredients

ST. JOHN'S WORT OIL

ST JOHN'S WORT FLOWERS, DRIED

A COPY OF THE WORKS OF VIRGIL

PEN AND PAPER

Rise at dawn and run a warm bath, adding six drops of St. John's wort oil. Relax for at least ten minutes, feeling the water envelop your body and freeing your mind of all other thoughts. Dry yourself, dress in bright colors, and eat a good breakfast. Wrap the flowers in some paper and keep them close to you all day. Take the book and, closing your eyes, let it fall open; place your finger somewhere on the open page. Write down the word that your finger lands on, then go on to read the whole paragraph. Draw a short line from the word you have written and write down the next word, or words, that comes into your head. Do this time and time again from the central word until the page is full. If you wish, you can do this part of the spell on the way to work. You will find that your brain is now ready to cope with anything!

1 As you have made an effort to rise at dawn, open a window and savor the sights and sounds of this magical time of the day.

2 When you have completed the first part of the spell, take your copy of Virgil to a chosen place or to work and let the pages fall open to find your word.

Golden Poppy An American

spell to bring you luck in money. The Californian poppy, with its bright

orange-yellow flowers, is also known as the "flower of gold." To Native

Americans it symbolizes the pleasures

of life. It is important, in this spell, that

you are not motivated by greed. If your

life is not all that you wish it to be, you

may need to think about making some important changes to enhance

your quality of life — remember that money alone cannot do this. Listen

to your heart and recognize the joys you have already experienced.

The gifts of the universe will rain down to further enhance your life.

Ingredients

A GOLD AND A SILVER COIN

A GOLDEN CANDLE

PEN AND PAPER

POPPY SEEDS

Start this spell late on a Thursday evening, with the waxing moon. Take the coins, charge them with the moon's light and call down a blessing from Jupiter for the work ahead. Light the candle and, by its light alone, write on the paper the reasons you need luck in money and the things you would do with it. Take your time, this is a very important list. Place the coins on each side of the candle and extinguish it. Place the paper under the candle and retire to bed. The following evening relight the candle and check your list — you may wish to amend it. If you feel happy with the contents, meditate for a few minutes on the candle's glow. Burn the list and collect the ashes. Mix these with the poppy seeds and the coins and plant them in a favorite spot.

1 **When you write your list, review your own life, its success and failure rate and the kind of input you need to make to bring luck in money.**

2 **As you burn the list in the candle flame, decide on one small gift you can give when your luck changes.**

Hive of Industry

Self-employment can be a tricky business at the best of times, so if you need to attract more work this spell might help. To get things moving

again, first analyze your own feelings and your attitude to what you are doing. You may find that your direction in life has changed and that you are no longer enjoying the work. We all need to eat and pay the bills, but true wealth is also reflected in the quality of our lives. When you are sure which path you wish to follow, use the new moon as a guide while performing this spell.

Ingredients

A WHITE CANDLE	A GLASS OF WATER
PEN AND INK	A BOTTLE
SOME PAPER	A SYMBOL OF YOUR
AN ENVELOPE	WORK

Light the candle – white for new beginnings – and let your mind think of the possibility of having work. Let your fear take form and then let it out by drawing it on paper. Put this in an envelope and seal it with candle wax. With pen and ink, write down positive thoughts about the work you need and place the paper in a glass of water. Turn the glass three times clockwise, so that the ink disperses. Strain the water containing your thoughts into a bottle. Place the envelope containing your fears in the freezer and leave it there for as long as you need. Take the bottle with you to a place with running water. Take the symbol of your work too and give it to the first person you meet on your way. Tip the water containing your thoughts into the running water and as you do so wish for luck in your future work.

1 **Brown is a good down-to-earth color to use for the ink in this spell. Watch as the ink disperses in the water and your thoughts dissolve.**

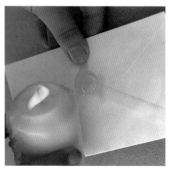

2 **You will need to let the candle burn for a few minutes before the wax is soft enough to seal the envelope.**

Golden Moon

A spell to make you receptive to all the opportunities within your touch. August to September, when the harvest is ready to be gathered in, is a good time to carry out this spell. It is important to prepare yourself, and a thorough cleansing ritual should be undertaken on the preceding three days. When you awake, take a bath to which you have added seven drops of your favorite essential oil and a teaspoon of salt, a symbol of immortality and protection. Find a room where the moon shines through a window; if this is not possible, a quiet place outside will work as well.

Ingredients

2 MIRRORS
3 ORANGE CANDLES
SOME ORANGE CORD
HONESTY SEEDS

*P*lace the mirrors opposite each other so that one mirror reflects a moonbeam back into the other. Take one of the candles and warm it, so that you can scratch your initials at the top in warm wax. Stand mid-way between the mirrors with the candles around you, so that you can see your initials on the candle. Light the candles and return to your place, holding the orange cord in your right hand and the honesty seeds in your left. Stand in the beam of moonlight and absorb its energy while the candle burns and frees the letters of your name. Turn around, clockwise, seven times, trailing the cord around you to gather the moonbeams about your body. Open yourself to receive all that comes your way. Then retire and sleep with the honesty seeds under your pillow. Bury them the next day.

1 Take care not to warm the candle too much or the wax will melt. A warm radiator is an ideal place to do this.

2 When you retire for the night hold a picture of the moonbeams coming to your body as you drift off to sleep.

Green Garland A Celtic

blessing charm to help you get back into the work market. Not having

work today is a depressing and sometimes debilitating experience. A

real sense of unleashed tension and spirit of

renewal can follow the simple task of carrying

out an age-old tradition. In times of trouble,

such as periods of unemployment, the spirit

needs as much care, if not more, than the

body. Reconnecting to the earth can heal great wounds and lay the

foundations of a new stability. Make your charm and journey when you

feel in greatest need and put your whole being into it.

Ingredients

A GARLAND OF SEASONAL LEAVES AND FLOWERS

A SMALL PIECE OF WOOD WITH
   YOUR NAME CARVED IN IT

SOME NATURAL TWINE, SUCH AS HESSIAN

Fashion a garland from the gifts of Mother Earth; ivy is a good ingredient no matter what time of year you perform this spell. The shape and size of the garland is not important; it could be a circle, a cross, or whatever takes your fancy. The most important thing is to spend time and dedication in making the symbol to the best of your ability and to make it a thing of beauty. Fasten the wood with your name on it to the garland using the natural twine. With your garland, make a special journey to a natural water source – an ancient well or spring, for example. Place your offering near the water and give thanks for your gifts. Sit for a while and soak in the magic and tranquility of the site. Let the peace pervade your mind.

1 **Use a trailing plant such as ivy, honeysuckle, or periwinkle, and tie it together with the twine to form your chosen shape.**

2 **Interlace flowers between the leaves, allowing a space to attach your personal talisman.**

Paper and Wax

Perform this spell for luck immediately before entering a competition or lottery, or at any time for surprise good fortune.

Work this charm on a waxing moon to give yourself the best chance of attracting success. We all have a secret wish to be the recipient of a windfall and imagine what we could do with it. Even the gift of a small amount of money can be a bonus, if it is used wisely. Remember, being motivated by selfishness is not a way to attract riches – a sincere desire to help others as well as yourself will have much more success.

Ingredients

A SILVER COIN

A RED CANDLE ANOINTED WITH FRANKINCENSE OIL

A PEN AND SCROLL OF PAPER

A PLENTY POT

A plenty pot is simply a store of money; it should only be used for the spell if in doing so its value is increased. This might include giving a share to a good cause or to a friend in need. Take the silver coin, charge it with the moon's rays, and light the anointed candle. Still holding the coin, write down the size of money gift you would make if you won a lot of money. Be honest! Seal the scroll with candle wax and place it at the bottom of the pot. Put the silver coin on top and add anything else you want to include, such as more money or a personal talisman. Sit with the candle, envisaging a glow of success surrounding your whole being. When you next enter a competition, take the coin with you and remember the candle's glow. Always place the original coin back in the plenty pot as well as adding more money to it.

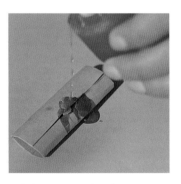

1 **Write down the size of your money gift. You may need to flatten the scroll to allow the coin to remain on the top of it. Seal with candle wax**

2 **Put your scroll into the plenty pot. Add your coin. With the plenty pot in view meditate on the candle.**

Seasonal Rites

Seven spells to help give you a sense of belonging and harmony with Mother Nature and her great gifts

Chapter Six

Lady Day

From the Druids, a ritual to welcome the living power of light. Lady Day (March 25th) or the day of the Return of the Goddess is still a "Quarter Day" in England, when

rents are often due. The Druids were the male or female magician-priests of the Celtic peoples. They often held celebrations on hilltops, known as beacons, when great fires were lit that became an interconnecting communication across the whole country. The Druids recognized the sun as a life-giving force and welcomed it into their lives. This ritual will reaffirm your connection in the circle of life.

Ingredients

A YELLOW FLOWER

SOME BEANS

The yellow flower is a symbol of your recognition of the great life-giving power of the sun, while the beans hold the promise of regeneration in the future for us all. On March 25th, make a special journey to a hilltop; if it is a site of an antiquity this will further enhance the ritual. The spirits of the past inhabit such places and with a little practice you will learn to recognize their presence and draw strength from them. Place the flower on the hilltop and turn toward the direction of the sun. Open your arms and welcome the sun into your life, pulling it down through your fingertips to warm your soul. Turn around three times in a clockwise direction, scattering the beans as you turn, and make your pledge for a more sustainable earth.

1 Choose the brightest yellow flower you can find, and take great care of it as you journey to the hilltop.

2 Put all your being into welcoming the sun and feel its warmth and life enter your deepest parts.

3 As you turn and make your pledge, use all your strength to scatter the beans as far afield as possible.

Sun and Earth

A spell for summer, the seasonal high point of the year, to invoke the energies of the sky and earth for lasting strength and happiness. Sympathetic magic has been used in many lands to celebrate the summer solstice. Midsummer-eve fires were lit to pay tribute to the power of the sun. In Lapland, families wove sun-rings from dried grass to honor the Sun Mother and ate "sun porridge," made from rich dairy products, to call for a blessing

on their reindeer herds. Midsummer magic is most suited to material rather than spiritual needs and desires.

Ingredients

SOME PAINT OR A PERMANENT PEN

A YELLOW PEBBLE OR CRYSTAL

A MARIGOLD PLANT

SEVEN STONES

If you wish to use this as a general spell for happiness, start at noon. If you have a particular request, such as love or money, dawn should be your starting time. The marigold is the flower of endurance that always turns its face toward the sun, following its path through the sky. It will give your spell longevity. Paint or use a permanent pen to draw your birth sign on the pebble or crystal. In your garden, or in a large pot of earth, make a hole and place the pebble at the bottom. Plant the marigold on top, placing the seven stones around it. As you work chant the following:

Sing me the song of seasons,
Show me the sun's delight,
Open my heart for your radiance,
Lead me toward the light.

Nurture the plant with care and do not pick its flowers.

1 **Embellish the pebble with your birth sign. This pebble, for example, is decorated with the glyph for the sun sign of Capricorn.**

2 **Fill the pot with earth or find a special place in the garden that will not be disturbed. Place the pebble in the earth.**

3 **Put the marigold plant on top of the pebble and draw the earth around it, chanting as you put the seven stones around the plant at regular intervals.**

Mexican Gift

This spell will bring the blessings of the sun into your life whatever the season. Witchcraft and magical rites have been practiced in Mexico since ancient times, a tradition that continues today with a mixture of Spanish and Aztec rituals that touch everyday life. Paper dolls, originally made from the bark of the *amate* (fig) tree, are used to represent the shadow or soul of a person, with the heart and stomach indicated by triangular cuts. To represent concepts or deities, the dolls are joined in groups of four and placed in colorful layers of black, yellow, red, or white.

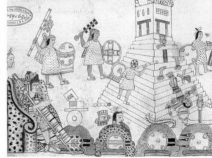

Ingredients

INCENSE STICKS

YELLOW PAPER

REEDS

A FEW FLOWERS

SOME RED CHILI PEPPERS

Work in the open air on a sunny day at any time of the year. Light an incense stick to work by and start to cut four joined figures from the yellow paper. Palm leaves are traditionally used in this spell, but reeds are more available and will work just as well. Take some of the reeds and form them into a the shape of a star. Decorate this star with flowers and the chili peppers shaped in the form of a cross. Tie them in place with reeds. Put the star in front of you on the earth and take the paper figures in your left hand and an incense stick in the right. Following the sun's path, circle your star seven times, wafting the incense over your offering and chanting the following words:

Brightest orb that lights the heaven,
Warm my soul and give me strength.

Bury the offering and take the paper figures into your home to remind you of the blessing.

1 The paper figures can be cut to represent a person of your choice, or just as a general symbol of a person.

2 Fresh reeds will bend and bind easily with each other to form a star shape. Fix the chilli in place.

3 Remain focussed on the star as you circle it seven times with the incense stick and make your blessing.

September Seal

This spell will reveal the true inner meaning of harvest and take you through the winter months. This is the time of year to harvest the raw

necessities of life, and to gather together, in your mind, those parts of your life that hold the most promise for the future. It is the Celtic month of Muin, sacred to the vine and the god Lugh, who represents wisdom and spiritual illumination. The autumnal equinox falls in September, when night and day are equal again. It is a time for inner equilibrium, a time for sorting things out and putting away "seeds" for the coming year.

Ingredients

AN EMPTY COFFEE CAN AND LID

SOME PAINT AND A BRUSH

DRIED GRAPE SEEDS

3 INCENSE STICKS

A MIRROR

SOME SAND

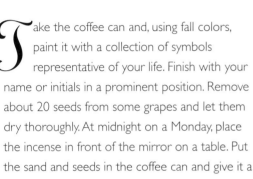

Take the coffee can and, using fall colors, paint it with a collection of symbols representative of your life. Finish with your name or initials in a prominent position. Remove about 20 seeds from some grapes and let them dry thoroughly. At midnight on a Monday, place the incense in front of the mirror on a table. Put the sand and seeds in the coffee can and give it a shake. Light the incense and put out all other lights. Sit in front of the mirror, but not too close. Place your right hand in the can and concentrate on the glow and reflected image. As you find a seed with your fingertips, reflect on it and decide if it is a part of your life that should be discarded or whether it is the fruit of a new beginning. Make two piles on the table, those you wish to keep and those you wish to discard – bury or burn the discarded seeds the next day.

I Use an undercoat of paint that will adhere to metal before you start to paint your designs. Let your imagination run wild with the symbols of your life as they form on the tin.

2 Gather all the ingredients close to you before you light the incense stick, and choose a place where you will not be disturbed to perform the rest of the spell.

Wheel of the Year

A spell for Yuletide, the turning point in the wheel of the year, when we look forward to better things. Underlying the customs associated with Christmas are the vestiges of ancient pagan rites that celebrated the winter solstice when nights began to get shorter again, bringing a promise of rebirth. At this time of the year, the Romans celebrated Saturnalia and decorated their homes with holly, laurel, and bay.

Holly is a symbol of life amid the death of winter. This is a ritual for the whole family and ideally it is carried out on the winter solstice, which is on December 21st.

Ingredients

NUTS AND FRUIT SUITABLE FOR BIRDS	RED RIBBON
DRIED FRUIT OR ORANGES	A CANDLE
HOLLY AND IVY	PEN AND PAPER
JUNIPER OIL AND OIL BURNER	

Rise before daybreak and greet the dawn, leaving a gift of nuts and fruit for the birds. Breakfast with your partner or family and include dried fruit or oranges in the meal to represent the sun. Go to gather or buy holly and ivy; traditionally holly is carried by the men and ivy by the women. Burn the juniper oil to rid the house of any bad spirits. Place a garland of ivy around the doorways inside the house, with a sprig of holly tied with red ribbon above the lintels. In the late afternoon, sit around the lighted candle and ask everyone to write or draw their regrets on the paper and then burn it in the flame. Take turns at speaking out your wishes for future happiness. Join hands and with collective concentration send out your wishes for the new year to be granted.

1 **Make this a very special breakfast, a ritual for throwing off the drear of the dark winter months and a start to new beginnings.**

2 **When you have collected the greenery tie it into sashes that can be draped and fixed around the doorways of your house.**

3 **As you sit together around the candle draw courage from your ritual and make the gathering a happy and intimate one.**

Green Dragon

Following the Chinese tradition, this spring spell will harness the courage to successfully tread in new directions, leaving you without doubt about your purpose. In Chinese myth, humans were clay statues made by Father-Heaven, who left them in the sun to dry. When rain began to fall, Father-Heaven quickly gathered them in to find shelter, but some were damaged. These became diseased humans, while the undamaged statues were the healthy. As in real life, so much of what happens is a matter of chance. By meeting this half way, we can at least have some control over our destiny.

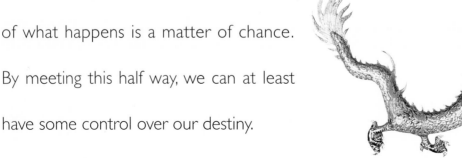

Ingredients

PAINT OR PERMANENT INK

SIX PALE-COLORED STONES

A CLOTH BAG

The Yang sign, an unbroken line, symbolizes "yes;" the Yin sign, two broken lines, represents "no." Paint the Yang sign on one side of each stone and the Yin sign on the other side of each stone. When ready, place the stones in the cloth bag. You are not trying to predict your future, just asking for guidance. Ask a straight forward question or a question containing two alternatives and then, without looking, throw the stones one at a time. When all the stones have been thrown, have a look – if you have an even number of yes and no answers, try again. If the same thing happens twice, rephrase the question. When the stones show mainly yes or mainly no then you should act accordingly. If all six stones show the same answer, act immediately.

1 Although you can buy the Yin/Yang symbols it is better if you make them yourself to make your magic stronger.

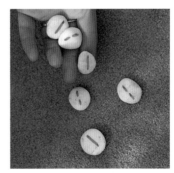

2 Make sure the stones are dry before you place them in the cloth bag, and settle yourself in peace and quiet before you start to throw them.

Crossroads

A Halloween spell to perform on one of the most magical nights of the year. The night of halloween or All Souls' Eve falls on October 31st and marks the onset of

the feast of Samhaine. The curtain between this world, the present, and the other-world, the past, is thinner at this time, making communication easier. This Halloween spell is intended to remind us of nature's transition from one part of the year to another as she withdraws for a winter rest. Taking time to celebrate the lives of lost friends and family can be a welcome release from our hectic modern lives.

Ingredients

5 PURPLE CANDLES

A MEMENTO, SUCH AS A PHOTOGRAPH, OF A PAST
  TIME OR LOVED ONE

2 HAZEL TWIGS, 1FT./30CM LONG

A LONG PIECE OF PURPLE CORD

Start this rite after 9 p.m. on Halloween. Light the candles and place them in a circle, large enough for you to walk around with ease. Put the memento in the center and cross the hazel twigs over it. Trail the cord in a circle outside the candles, then step among the candles and close the circle of cord behind you. Laying aside the twigs, pick up your memento and sit for a few moments, composing yourself. When ready, take a hazel twig in each hand. Lay them across each index finger with the thumb resting lightly on top; they should be able to wiggle slightly. Walk slowly around the circle clockwise, thinking of the spirits of all those who have gone before, and of the latent rebirth that takes place in the spring. If your hazel rods cross, this means that other energies are present so let your love go out to them.

1 Ensure that the candles are placed in a large safe circle, and that the hot wax will not do any harm while you are meditating.

2 The hazel twigs should rest in your hands with as little grip as possible as though they are becoming an extension to your body.

Counter Charms

A little magic to banish negative energies from your life. But remember, work these spells with honorable intentions, never malice

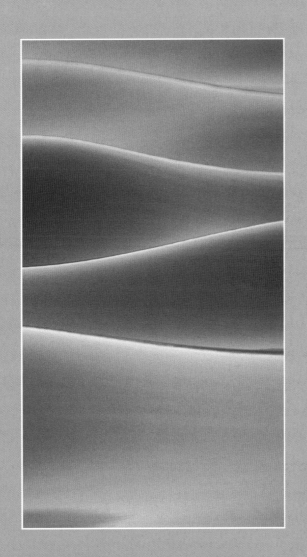

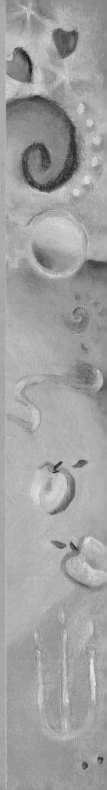

Chapter Seven

Sea Wishes

A Scandinavian tradition to evoke the spirits of the sea and help you break bad habits, such as smoking or over-indulging in food or drink. You will need to journey to the coast to harness the potent magic of the ocean and its tides. Pagan-

ism survived much longer in Scandinavia than in other parts of Europe, and these ancient beliefs and ceremonies have been passed on to this day. The runes, a secret language, are an intrinsic part of Scandinavian magic – with their aid, perform this spell as the tide is going out and with the cycle of the waning moon.

Ingredients

A SYMBOL OF WHAT YOU WISH TO GIVE UP

A SMALL PURSE OR POUCH

A PIECE OF DRIFTWOOD

A SHARP KNIFE

Keep the symbol of your bad habit in a purse or pouch close to your body. When you get to the shore find a piece of driftwood and, with the knife, etch the runic symbols of strength and protection onto it, all the while thinking positively about breaking your habit. When the tide is going out, remove your shoes and wade up to your knees. Hold the runes in your left hand and walk in an counterclockwise circle seven times. On each circuit, pick up a some small treasure from the seabed and place it in the purse. On the last turn, gently place your driftwood on a wave and watch it travel away from you. Take a piece of seaweed home with you and hang it outside your door to remind you of the task in hand. Take the contents of the purse and bury it in your yard.

1 The best place to find driftwood is above the tide line. Choose a piece that is reasonably dry so you are able to carve symbols on it.

The runic symbol for strength.

The runic symbol for protection.

2 As you place seaweed on your door, keep a mental picture of the ritual you have performed and your determination to drop the bad habit.

Adverse Affections

A little magic from Italy to deter a rival from moving in on your relationship. Coping with the unprincipled advances of a competitor for your

partner's affection can be soul-destroying, even if the feelings are not being reciprocated. It is important to keep your head so that you can think clearly and plan the path ahead with a little magic to ease the way. Remember to make sure your own motives are virtuous or the whole thing may backfire. Work in secret on a Tuesday night with the waning moon to get things moving and restore harmony in the relationship.

Ingredients

A BLUE CANDLE

CLOVE OIL AND OIL BURNER

A BAY LEAF

Bay and cloves are both plants that are strongly associated with protection, as is the color blue. Gently warm the candle, so that the wax becomes soft. Score the name of your adversary (if you know it), or a symbol for that person into the wax. As you work, tell the person that you wish him or her no harm, only success in finding love with someone unattached rather than with your partner. Burn the clove oil and light the candle, watching as the name or symbol is consumed. At the same time, hold the bay leaf in the flame for just a few seconds, wishing your love to be true to you only and to have nothing more to do with the other person. Keep the bay leaf safe, and the next time you cook an appropriate meal for your partner, use it as seasoning. When the candle has burned sufficiently and there is no sign of the name left in the wax, take the remains and leave it in a garbage can positioned at a crossroads.

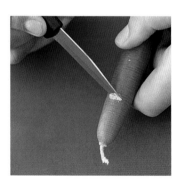

1 While you are warming the candle get all the other ingredients ready. You only need to press lightly to etch your symbol into the warmed candle.

2 Move the bay leaf back and forth across the candle flame so that it does not burn. Make your wish.

Tree Spirits

A Celtic charm to rid your dwelling place of bad spirits. Trees held a special significance to the Celts, but the following seven were sacred and especially magical: birch, alder, willow, oak, holly, hazel, and apple. Relics of ancient tree worship still survive today – many people still

touch wood for luck. It is quite acceptable to collect the wood for this charm over a period of time and reserve it in a special place. However, collecting it on the day of the spell can focus and add extra purpose to your mission. A Monday with the waning moon is a good time to perform this charm.

Ingredients

SEVEN SMALL PIECES OF WOOD, ONE FROM
  EACH OF THE SACRED TREES
AN UNWANTED ITEM FROM YOUR HOME, OR A SYMBOL
  OF YOUR HOME
A STOUT WHITE CANDLE

Rise early, take a cleansing bath and dress in white. A grove of trees is the best place for this ritual but a spot near one of the Celtic sacred trees will work as well. Collect the wood or take it with you. Put down your unwanted item or symbol and the candle. Arrange the seven pieces of wood around them and light the candle. Pick up the first piece of wood and chant;

> *Sacred tree of ancient time,*
> *Protect and guard my own abode.*

Replace the wood and blow out the candle. Re-light it and pick up the second piece of wood, repeating the chant. Do this with all the pieces of wood. Bury the unwanted item, then place the candle over the spot and light it while you reflect upon the magic of the trees. Take the pieces of sacred wood home and thread them onto a cord. Keep this in a prominent place in your home.

l **If you are working outside choose a sheltered spot for the candle so the flame is not extinguished.**

2 **As you thread the charmed wood, take note of all the differences between each piece. Hang the wood in a prominent position in your home.**

Witch's Candle

With its roots in Greece, a spell to relieve you of the attentions of an unwanted lover. If you feel you have done everything in your power to ease the split from a partner you no longer wish to have around you, without wishing to do that person harm, this spell may help. Mullein was used by Ulysses to protect himself against the trickery of the witch, Circe. Its use in spells earned mullein the name of "witch's candle" – an appropriate description of the soft yellow flowers that grow on a steeple-like stem up to 6ft./2m tall. The stem was sometimes dried, dipped in tallow, and used as a taper.

Ingredients

MULLEIN OIL AND OIL BURNER

A LOCK OF UNWANTED PARTNER'S HAIR

SOME OF YOUR NAIL FILINGS

SMALL CHINA BOWL

A BLUE CANDLE

SOME THREAD

Burn mullein oil in your house all day to start the protective influence and give strength to your spell. In the evening, during a waning moon, in a place you will not be disturbed, mix together your nail filings and the lock of hair in the bowl. If you do not have, or do not want to get a lock of the person's hair (he or she might think of it as an encouragement), simply write their name on a piece of paper and cut it into pieces. Stir everything together with

your right index finger and chant:

The seeds of this love have withered and died,
Set me free to live and thrive.

Light the candle and pluck the hair or paper from your nail filings. Add the nail filings to a little mullein oil and burn so your essence fills the atmosphere. Tie the hair into a bundle with the thread and seal it with wax. Then burn or bury it.

1 **Repeat the chant several times as you stir the ingredients in the pot. It will add strength to your spell.**

2 **When you have added the filings to the oil, bind the hair or paper round and round with thread and then seal it.**

Family Rift

A spell to deal with family members who are making familial relationships difficult. Performing a ritual as a family can often strengthen bonds and emphasize the benefit of working together as a collective. In early times, it was essential to pull together just to ensure basic existence. With the

abundance of material possessions in the Western world today, we often lose sight of the more spiritual aspect of relationships and the need to confirm them. Work on a Monday, the day of the family, and with a waxing moon because you wish to restore balance.

Ingredients

A SYMBOL OF THE RIFT OR GRIEVANCE
OF EACH MEMBER OF THE FAMILY

A SPADE

A SWEET-SMELLING, PINK ROSE

se gentle persuasion to get the whole family to participate – heavy-handed tactics will have the opposite effect. If anyone among you cannot find a suitable object as a symbol, they can jot down their thoughts and feelings on paper just as well. In your yard (a large pot filled with soil can act as a substitute) stand in a circle and take turns to dig a hole in the earth, passing the shovel around the group clockwise. Taking turns, with the oldest going first, bury your symbols in the ground, making a farewell to your sorrows. Together, completely cover them with earth and plant the rose, the flower of love, on the spot. R. "Great Maidens Blush" and R. "Celeste" are good choices for the garden, with R. "Baby Masquerade" for a pot. Take turns to water the rose and bless your planting.

1 When you take turns to bury the symbols, do so in silence and take a moment to reflect on your spell.

2 Join hands to make a farewell to your joint sorrows, and then smile at each other as you plant the rose.

Breaching the Gap

A Germanic spell intended to heal a breach in a relationship. You must be perfectly honest; if you have been the cause of the split, an apology is the first step to take in resolving the situation. Even if you were not the  cause of the argument and you sincerely want to patch things up, get rid of your own anger and resentment with some gentle meditation before you resort to magic. The rose is a symbol of love, dedicated to Venus. Carry out this spell on any day of the week and with a waxing or waning moon because you are giving or taking, depending on which way you look at things.

Ingredients

RED AND WHITE CLIMBING ROSES

RED AND WHITE RIBBON

RED WINE

3 TSP. ROSE WATER

Sit peacefully with a picture of your partner in your mind and consider all his or her good attributes and why you love that person. Try to remain in this position until all your negative feelings have left you. Place your right index finger on your brow and focus on sending out loving feelings to your partner. In your garden, plant the red and white climbing roses next to each other and intertwine them, sealing them with the red and white ribbon. If you do not have a garden, use indoor ivy plants, tying a red ribbon around one and a white ribbon around the other. On your next meeting, serve your partner a glass of red wine to which you have added three teaspoons of rosewater. Don't be aloof or cold. When the ice has broken, and you feel the time is right and the healing energies have worked, show your partner your handiwork.

1 **Close your eyes while you let tension leave your body. Open them as you place your finger on your brow and visualize your love for your partner reaching outward.**

2 **Use the ribbon to encourage your plants to intertwine, and remove it once they are growing together.**

3 **Be calm and relaxed as you serve the wine and wait for its effect before you show your partner your work.**

Heartsease

From France comes a spell to help mend a broken heart. Heartsease, or wild pansy, has long been associated with affairs of the heart. It has flowers of three colors — white, yellow, and purple — and became known as the "tricolor." In the language of flowers, these colors represent memories, loving thoughts,

and souvenirs; the plant was given as a gift to ease the heartbreak of separation. If you are feeling lonely and rejected, this spell will help to bring comfort and make way for new beginnings. A waxing moon should accompany this spell.

Ingredients

YOUR FAVORITE ESSENTIAL OIL

AN ORANGE SILK SCARF

3 HEARTSEASE OR PANSY PLANTS

A CLOVE OF GARLIC

A PIECE OF PAPER WITH YOUR NAME ON IT

A POT AND SOME SOIL

Take a cleansing bath to which you have added some of your favorite oil, then dress with care. Wear the orange scarf tied close to you skin – around your waist if you feel shy of wearing such a bright color – or match it to your outfit and wear it boldly draped around your neck. It symbolizes the determination to succeed and will remind you of this each time you sense its presence. When buying the heartsease or pansy plants, choose the brightest colors you can find. At home, wrap the clove of garlic in the paper with your name on it; garlic is the plant of power. Place this in the bottom of the pot and cover with the soil. Plant the three pansies together on top and water well. Put them on a well-lit windowsill. As you tend and nurture the plants, your heart will mend and your *joie de vie* will return.

1 **As you wear the wonderful orange of optimism, take any compliment that comes your way with good heart – enjoy it!**

2 **Make a special journey with your orange talisman to collect the plants. When you return write your name on the paper and enclose the garlic.**

3 **As you have placed the paper in the pot think of all that life has to offer you and of the beauty you are nurturing in your pot.**

Three for Luck

If you need a little luck then try one of these three spells to attract some good fortune

Chapter Eight

Spectrum of Light

A seven-day spell to attract the beneficial power of the spirits, this can also be performed in unison with other spells to make them more

potent. The spell combines the magic of herbs, crystals, and candles to bring special luck in any task you perform. For each day of the week a different color is combined with its associations to draw upon the beneficial influences of the moon or the sun. It can be worked at any time of the day or year, starting on any day of the week you choose, but you must continue for seven days.

Ingredients

SEVEN CANDLES, ONE EACH OF
THE COLORS GIVEN BELOW
FRESH OR DRIED HERBS, AS GIVEN
FOR THE DAYS OF THE WEEK BELOW
FRANKINCENSE AND INCENSE BURNER
A CRYSTAL

On whichever day you start this spell choose an appropriately colored candle and matching herb from the list (right). Light the candle and the incense burner containing the frankincense, and sprinkle some of the herb into it. Hold the crystal in your outstretched hand and let the moon's or sun's rays pass through it so that they shed light onto the herbs in the burner. Call down the spirits with this beam and ask them to bestow luck on you and your task.

DAY	COLOR	MATCHING HERB
Sunday	Orange	Marjoram or catnip
Monday	White	Basil or lavender
Tuesday	Red	Nutmeg or rue
Wednesday	Yellow	Sage or ginger
Thursday	Purple	Bay or orris
Friday	Blue	Fennel or clove
Saturday	Green	Parsley or thyme

1 Take in the piquancy of each herb you burn, letting it fill your mind with remembered snatches of time or of things to come.

2 Take a few moments to meditate before you call down the sun's or moon's rays to the crystal in your palm.

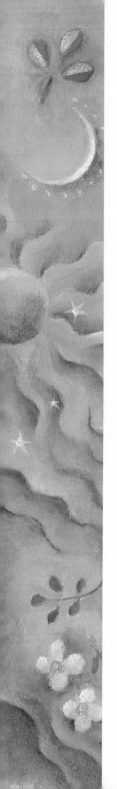

Sitting in Clover

Psychic protection, luck, and happiness are all included in this charm from the Druids. In Christian times a three-leafed clover was seen as a symbol of the Trinity and a four-leafed clover as a symbol of the cross. This may have developed from the pagan belief that clover was particularly lucky for women. The three leaves represented the goddess in her three manifestations, as the young woman, the mother, and the old crone of wisdom. Although all clover was endowed with magical properties, finding a four-leafed clover has always been especially lucky.

Ingredients

THREE PIECES OF CLOVER

THREE SILVER CANDLES

THIS BOOK OF SPELLS

SOME CLEAR TAPE

Carry out this spell on any day and at any hour. Collect three pieces of clover – the three-leafed variety will work beautifully but if you find a four-leafed clover, it will bring extra special luck to your spell. Light the three candles and place the clover in front of them. The clover should be flat so that the shape of the leaves is visible. Extend your fingers and put your hands over the clover. Focus on the candle's glow and picture yourself in a field of sweetly scented, red and white clover flowers, bathed in a soft silver light that lifts all cares from you and sends them soaring away. Rest a little, then extinguish the candles. Press the clover very flat and tape it inside the cover of this spell book to keep luck with you at all times.

1 **Light the three candles and place the clover in front of them. The clover should be flat so the shape of the leaves is visible.**

2 **Relax and extend your fingers to cover the three clover leaves.**

3 **Press the clover very flat and tape it to the inside cover of your spell book to bring you luck.**

Bundle of Joy

From the Native American tradition, a cache of magical charms to attract luck. Natural objects, such as herbs, bones, and wood, which embody the energies and spiritual power latent in humans, were collected and tied in cloth or leather to form medicine bundles. The contents of these were sacred to the tribe. Personal medicine bundles were also collected and their contents were strictly private. When the owner died, the medicine bundle was burned so his or her spirit would have no ties to this world. Create your own bundle to keep luck at your side.

Ingredients

SEEDS, STONES, CRYSTALS, FEATHERS,
WOOD, AND ANY OTHER NATURAL SUBSTANCE
NATURAL CLOTH AND THONG

The collection of objects for your medicine bundle should be gathered over a period of time. It is better to include different items that attract you in an unconscious way than to make hasty decisions; your medicine bundle might have to last for many years. Each time you visit the countryside, pay special attention to your surroundings; notice the wealth of nature and look closely for things that you might normally miss. Dry any fresh plants or herbs collected, after familiarizing yourself with their scent and texture. When you have made your choice, wrap them in the cloth and secure it with the thong. The bundle can be large or small. If it is large, keep it in a safe, personal space in your home. A small bundle can be worn around the neck to remind you of the luck you carry with you.

Good Luck and Best Wishes!

1 When collecting items for your bundle treat Mother Nature with care. Let the items you collect give you a deeper understanding of all the amazing things that surround you.

2 You can choose any color cloth or thong to make your bundle as long as it is made from a natural substance.

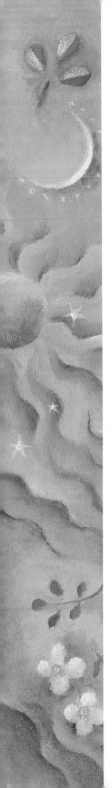

Index